Understanding Male Homosexual Problems

An Introduction for Latter-day Saints

by
Jason Park

CENTURY PUBLISHING
SALT LAKE CITY, UTAH
1997

Understanding Male Homosexual Problems: An Introduction for Latter-day Saints

Third printing 2001

Copyright © 1997 by Century Publishing

This work is not a publication of The Church of Jesus Christ of Latter-day Saints. The views expressed herein are the responsibility of the author and do not necessarily represent the position of the Church or of Century Publishing.

ISBN 0–941846–08–3

Printed in the United States of America.

Introduction

This booklet provides a brief introduction to the subject of homosexuality in the context of the gospel of Jesus Christ. It may be helpful to men who want to follow Christ and resolve their homosexual feelings, and also to wives, parents, siblings, friends, and Church leaders who want to help. Homosexual problems are difficult to overcome and those who are the most successful are those who clearly understand the task ahead of them and receive support from their family and friends.

Individuals can resolve their homosexual problems and live in harmony with the gospel. The author knows this first-hand because he has experienced such changes in his own life. The solution to homosexual attractions is *not* to simply suppress the feelings and control the behavior through will-power. The goal is to *resolve* the inner conflicts that created the homosexual attractions. Although homosexual behavior can be stopped in the short term by exercising willpower, the unmet emotional and social needs won't go away until they are fulfilled in nonsexual ways. As men resolve the underlying causes, the unwanted impulses will diminish or disappear.

This booklet is written about male homosexual issues. Some of the information may also be helpful to women who struggle with lesbianism and some may not. More research needs to be done on women's issues to better determine causes and solutions.

This booklet is only an introduction. It briefly addresses the following questions:
♦   What is homosexuality?
♦   Why are men attracted to other men?
♦   Can homosexual problems be resolved?
♦   How can homosexual problems be resolved?

For further information, read the following books:

Resolving Homosexual Problems: A Guide for LDS Men by Jason Park. Written to Latter-day Saint men who want to resolve their homosexual feelings, this book provides practical solutions to resolve the personal problems they face.

Helping LDS Men Resolve their Homosexual Problems: A Guide for Family, Friends, and Church Leaders by Jason Park. Since a man's journey out of homosexuality will be easier if he has the support of others, this book gives family, friends, and priesthood leaders ideas on supporting someone they love.

What Is Homosexuality?

This chapter defines homosexuality, including attractions, identity, and behavior. The chapter then presents LDS doctrines concerning homosexuality, including the distinction between homosexual thoughts and behavior, and the importance of overcoming both. Finally, it offers correct information about homosexual problems.

Description

Homosexual problems include erotic thoughts, feelings, and behaviors directed toward the same gender. The psychological community uses the term *homosexuality* to refer to the entire complex that includes attractions, feelings, desires, sexual behavior, identity, and all its associated aspects, such as problems with masculinity, self-perception, emotional dependencies, and relationship issues.

These problems should not be confused with a healthy emotional and social interest in persons of the same gender. Homo*emotional* and homo*social* interests are healthy as long as they are not excessive and do not develop an erotic dimension. When same-gender interests are eroticized, they become homo*sexual*.

I use the term *homosexual* as an adjective to describe a person's feelings, thoughts, or behavior, but not as a noun to describe the person. The terms *gay* (referring to men) and *lesbian* (referring to women) include not only personal feelings and behaviors, but also describe a political, cultural, and social identity.

Homosexuality may include sexual feelings or attractions without sexual behavior or it may include complete emotional and sexual involvement. It cannot be identified simply by the presence or absence of outward sexual behavior.

Attractions

Homosexual attractions develop over time and almost always without any conscious choice. At some point in the man's life, he realized he was sexually attracted to other men.* These attractions can be a major source of frustration, because in spite of his best efforts to get rid of them, he continues to have compelling sexual thoughts toward other men. These inner attractions may be intense and may consume a great deal of his thoughts and energy. If the sexual attractions are not resolved, they can grow into obsessions that interfere with his ability to function at work and at home, and can be destructive spiritually. Homosexual attractions are usually more compelling than attractions toward the opposite sex because they spring from more than sexual desires—they are attempts to fill unmet emotional and social needs.

Many men report they first noticed these attractions before puberty—before they felt or understood sexual feelings. The feelings were not inherently sexual, but at some point became eroticized. The needs involved are normal social and emotional needs that everyone has, but have become confused and sexualized toward the same gender. The attractions are actually attempts to meet the emotional and identity needs that have not yet been met in his life. As a child, some part of his normal developmental process was stopped and interfered with his ability to develop a heterosexual orientation. Ironically, sexual intimacy will not fill the needs. They should not be ignored (the conservative mistake)

---

* As explained in the introduction, the focus of this booklet is on male homosexual problems. Although much of this information can also be helpful to women who have lesbian issues, don't assume that all the theories or strategies presented here will work for them.

nor eroticized (the liberal mistake), but should be filled through legitimate, nonsexual means. Here, then, is the irony. Homosexuality itself has little to do with sex; the needs are not homo*sexual*, but homo*emotional*.

Identity

Many men with homosexual attractions report they felt "different" as boys but didn't know why. For such a boy, the pain of growing up with homosexual attractions was not so much the pain of being attracted to boys, but the feelings of being different. These feelings of being different may have become a self-fulfilling prophecy as he separated himself from the very boys he needed to bond with. He may have longed to feel he was on par with other boys, but this longing only widened the gulf between him and the rest of the guys. Feeling different may create a mindset that can have a tremendous impact on a boy's self-perception and development. When other children sense this hesitancy, they often attack it, which only confirms to the boy that he is different. Thus, he withdraws from other boys to defend himself from the pain.

He knew his attractions were not right because of the "fag" jokes he heard, so he learned to keep the feelings to himself, creating further problems of isolation and secrecy, which are powerful forces that keep homosexual problems from being resolved. When the rest of the male world is normally attracted to females, he may have wondered why he was abnormally attracted to males. Knowing these attractions were in conflict with his religious beliefs and society's norms, he realized his innermost feelings were wrong and since he didn't choose to have these feelings, he may have wondered if there was something inherently wrong with him. This likely created an internal struggle as he desperately tried to understand the unnatural feelings and make sense of them in terms of his own internal values and religious beliefs.

A person's identity is an accumulation of self-perceptions. He may come to believe he was born with homosexual feelings which are part of his core identity. He may become convinced that if he is ever to be at peace with himself, he must submit to his desires, even if it means rejecting (or at least ignoring) his religious beliefs and personal values. When a person "comes out of the closet" and identifies himself as homosexual, he often feels relief for two reasons. First, after suffering so much frustration and pain, he is relieved to have finally made a difficult decision and he may interpret this temporary relief as confirmation that he has made the right choice. Secondly, he may find the acceptance and emotional closeness with other homosexual men that he had not been able to find previously. If he accepts a homosexual identity, it will have far-reaching implications and profoundly influence how he thinks and acts. In addition to resolving the homosexual issues, he will have the additional challenge of correcting misperceptions about himself.

Behavior

Homosexual attractions can be strong if he entertains sexual fantasies. Because of the intensity of these sexual desires, he may have participated in sexual activities to fill the void he feels. However, this causes further confusion, leading him to believe that the needs are sexual rather than emotional. In a desperate attempt to satisfy these building tensions, he may have become involved in sexual activities that provide a temporary gratification of the sex drive, but leave him with deeper feelings of emptiness, loneliness and frustration. Rather than satisfying his real needs for acceptance and companionship, the sexual behavior only intensifies the needs. One of the greatest tragedies of homosexuality is the unawareness in most men that their needs are emotional. All they know is that they are sexually attracted to other men and they seek sexual contacts, which ironically do not fill their need for love from a friend.

Not all men find themselves involved in sexual behavior. Some have participated in only limited behavior and others have remained chaste in spite of their intense attractions. Those who have not acted on their desires will have a much easier journey out of homosexuality because of it.

Homosexuality is symptomatic of other problems

One of the reasons homosexual problems are difficult to address is that they are not the real problem. Focusing too much on homosexual problems can actually be misleading, since they are symptoms of deeper struggles, such as rejection, envy, abuse, self-perception, gender identity, distrust, or fear. However, men who have homosexual problems seldom recognize this because they are masters at hiding the real issues in their lives. They hide them from others and even from themselves. Many of these issues are common and others vary from person to person. Once a man identifies the causes of his painful hunger he can learn ways to feed the hunger in appropriate, nonsexual ways. Once he resolves the underlying problems, he will find that the homosexual problems resolve themselves.

Why is homosexuality a problem?

A sexual *attraction* toward other men distorts healthy, loving relationships and steers a man away from the blessings that can be found in marriage and family relationships. It diverts capable priesthood holders from the roles of husband and father. Homosexual *behavior* is of particular concern because it violates God's commandments and blocks his eternal progress.

Gospel teachings regarding homosexuality

God created us as male or female (see Genesis 1:27). He wants men and women to join with each other under the covenant of marriage to procreate and fulfill their eternal destiny. In His eternal plan, there are no classifications of *homosexuals, bisexuals,* or *heterosexuals*. We are all on this earth having a human experience with various challenges to overcome so we can become the true men, women, priesthood holders, wives, husbands, mothers, and fathers that God wishes us to be.

Homosexual feelings

A 1991 letter issued by the First Presidency to all members of the Church stated, "there is a distinction between [1] immoral thoughts and feelings and [2] participating in either immoral heterosexual or any homosexual behavior."[1] An individual usually has no fault in the emergence of the feelings that trigger the homosexual attractions. Since he made no conscious choice for them, he should not feel guilty for having them. However, he can choose how he responds to the attractions and should not deliberately feed the feelings by fantasizing and turning them into lustful thoughts. The First Presidency letter continued, "However, such thoughts and feelings, regardless of their causes, can and should be overcome. . . ."[2] The individual is responsible for his agency in the thoughts he entertains. In an article in the *Ensign* magazine about same-gender attraction, Elder Dallin H. Oaks clarified that "although immoral thoughts are less serious than immoral behavior, such thoughts also need to be resisted and repented of because we know that 'our thoughts will also condemn us' (Alma 12:14). Immoral thoughts (and the less serious feelings that lead to them) can bring about behavior that is sinful."[3]

Sexual behavior

The scriptures are clear in condemning homosexual practices. We read in Romans, "For this cause God gave them up unto *vile* affections: for even their women did *change* the *natural* use into that which is *against nature*: And likewise also the men, leaving the *natural* use of the woman, burned in their *lust* one toward another; *men with men* working that which is *unseemly*, and receiving in themselves that recompense of their *error* which was meet" (Romans 1:26–27; emphasis added).

President Gordon B. Hinckley stated, "Prophets of God have repeatedly taught through the ages that practices of homosexual relations, fornication, and adultery are grievous sins. Sexual relations outside the bonds of marriage are forbidden by the Lord."[4] The First Presidency declared, "The Lord's law of moral conduct is abstinence outside of lawful marriage and fidelity within marriage. Sexual relations are proper only between husband and wife appropriately expressed within the bonds of marriage. Any other sexual contact, including fornication, adultery, and homosexual and lesbian behavior, is sinful."[5]

Overcome thoughts and behavior

The 1991 letter from the First Presidency further stated, "We commend and encourage those who are overcoming inappropriate thoughts and feelings. We plead with those involved in such behavior to forsake it. We love them and pray for them. We are confident that through repentance and obtaining needed help, they can experience the peace that comes from conforming their lives to God's teachings."[6] President Gordon B. Hinckley said, "Our hearts reach out to those who struggle with feelings of affinity for the same gender. We remember you before the Lord, we sympathize with you, we regard you as our brothers and our sisters.

However, we cannot condone immoral practices on your part any more than we can condone immoral practices on the part of others."[7]

Elder Dallin H. Oaks said, "The struggles of those who are troubled by same-sex attraction are not unique. There are many kinds of temptations, sexual and otherwise. The duty to resist sin applies to all of them."[8]

Help those who are trying to overcome

After speaking in a general conference on the subject of same-gender attraction, President Gordon B. Hinckley said, "Having said this, I desire now to say with emphasis that our concern for the bitter fruit of sin is coupled with Christlike sympathy for its victims, innocent or culpable. We advocate the example of the Lord, who condemned the sin, yet loved the sinner. We should reach out with kindness and comfort to the afflicted, ministering to their needs and assisting them with their problems."[9]

Elder Dallin H. Oaks said that "each member of Christ's church has a clear-cut doctrinal responsibility to show forth love and to extend help and understanding. Sinners, as well as those who are struggling to resist inappropriate feelings, are not people to be cast out but people to be loved and helped (see 3 Ne. 18:22–23, 30, 32)."[10] Elder Oaks continued, "Church leaders are sometimes asked whether there is any place in The Church of Jesus Christ of Latter-day Saints for persons with homosexual or lesbian susceptibilities or feelings. Of course there is. The degree of difficulty and the pattern necessary to forgo behavior and to control thoughts will be different with different individuals, but the message of hope and the hand of fellowship offered by the Church is the same for all who strive."[11] Elder Oaks further explained that "all should understand that persons (and their family members) struggling with the burden of same-sex attraction are in special need of the love and encouragement that is a clear responsibility of Church members, who have signified by covenant their willingness 'to bear one another's burdens' (Mosiah 18:8) 'and so fulfil the law of Christ' (Gal. 6:2)."[12]

How many people have homosexual problems?

Pro-gay advocates claim that 10% of the population has a homosexual orientation. More conservative estimates place the figure at 1–3%. However, if you include everyone who has had a homosexual experience since puberty, the numbers are more in the neighborhood of 5–10%.[13]

Whatever the numbers, homosexual problems are significant and touch the lives of many people. If we use the conservative figure of 5%, of the ten million members of the Church there are 500,000 who have some degree of homosexual problems. And if you count their parents, spouses, brothers and sisters, it could add up to *nearly three million members of the Church directly affected.*[14] Add to that grandparents, uncles, aunts, and concerned Church leaders, and you can see that many more people are affected.

The truth about men who have homosexual feelings

Men do not choose to have homosexual feelings. These attractions usually develop because social and emotional needs were not met in the developmental years. It is not a matter of choice, except for a few people who just enjoy being different, which we find in any behavioral group.

Men do not develop homosexual problems because they are afraid of women. In reality, relationships with women generally have little to do with homosexual problems; instead, they have to do with relationships with men.

They are not effeminate men with limp wrists who speak with a lisp. Contrary to popular belief, only a small minority of men with homosexual problems displays effeminate man-

nerisms. Likewise, many men who have effeminate character-
istics have no homosexual problems. It is misleading to
assume that effeminate traits indicate homosexual problems.

They do not dress in women's clothing. Cross-dressing
(transvestism) is not typical of those who have homosexual
problems. About 80% of cross-dressers are heterosexual.[15]

*They do not feel they are women trapped in men's bod-
ies.* Very few men with homosexual tendencies feel this way.
Men who want hormone treatment or surgery to become
women are referred to as transsexuals.

For further reading

"Same-Gender Attraction," Dallin H. Oaks, *Ensign*, Oct.
    1995, pp. 7–14.

Why Are Men Attracted to Other Men?

Many factors contribute to the development of homosexual attractions. Dr. Elizabeth Moberly, author of *Homosexuality: A New Christian Ethic*, explained, "[M]any things are capable of causing the disruption in attachment that underlies the homosexual condition. It is not a question of one particular cause leading of necessity to one particular effect."[16] It is difficult to develop theories about the origins of homosexual attractions because no single theory fits every situation. Although there are some commonalities among people, there are no constants. Factors are different from person to person, or at least individual reactions to the same factors vary. Humans are complex beings and our behaviors are the result of many complex interactions.[17] This chapter discusses how personality, biological inheritance, and developmental experiences influence the development of homosexual problems.

Personality

Before we were born, we existed as spirits, and before that as unique intelligences (see Abraham 3:21–23). Our personalities were not created at physical birth, but have been developing long before that. It is no wonder that every person has different likes, desires, dreams, and moods. We see ourselves and the world in different ways and each of us hopes for something a little different from life. One child may be content with the affection he receives from his parents, while his sibling who receives the same attention feels a deficit and requires more. Some children seem content to play by themselves, while others who have many friends seem to need even more.

Many men with homosexual attractions have a heightened

sense of emotional sensitivity which can make them vulnerable to emotional hurt when their high expectations are not met. Since we all have different needs and perspectives on life, it is easy to see why two people in the same situation will react differently. For one person, a negative situation may be manageable, while for another it is a devastating crisis.

Biology

Science has not shown that homosexuality is an inborn or biologically-determined characteristic. Biology may play some small role in influencing behavior or feelings. Some people seem susceptible to particular actions and may be drawn toward them or become addicted to them more easily than other people.[18] One person may be able to dabble with gambling, while another becomes a compulsive gambler. Some may drink only socially, while others have an unusual attraction to alcohol. Studies indicate that genetics may be a factor in susceptibilities to some behavior-related disorders, such as aggression, obesity, or alcoholism. Likewise, there are theories that claim biological predispositions influence the development of homosexual attractions when other life experiences are also present.[19]

Beyond such predispositions, some scientists search for more direct genetic causes—a gene or chromosome that actually determines sexual orientation. News reports on these studies have misrepresented the facts. If you read the reports published by the researchers, you find that they admit their findings are not conclusive. Most scientists today give genetic theories little credibility.[20]

Regardless of the role that genetics play in the development of sexual attractions, such attractions are changeable and treatable. Each individual has control over his destiny. Each child of God has moral agency and can determine the course of his life. Regardless of any biological thread, thousands of men who struggle with homosexual attractions have made changes in their lives for the better.

Developmental experiences

Professionals agree that environment influences a child in significant ways. His family, friends, society, and his experiences influence how he feels, how he views life, and how he acts. Dr. William Consiglio refers to this myriad of social and psychological factors as a "conspiracy of factors," meaning that many factors "conspired" or came together in the right amounts at the right time to divert sexual desires in a developing boy toward other boys.[20] Some of these factors include the boy's relationship with his family and peers, his ability to identify with masculinity, the degree to which his emotional needs are fulfilled, his feelings of self-worth, and early sexual experiences.

Relationship with father

When I first tried to understand how my homosexual attractions had developed, I didn't think my family was dysfunctional. We loved each other and my father didn't beat us. We lived in peace and love and were active in the Church. However, I later came to realize that these good things did not guarantee that all my emotional needs would be met.

It is important that a boy have a healthy emotional relationship with his father or with another significant male. (This is much more than Sigmund Freud's theory that a homosexual male child is the product of a strong mother and a passive, indifferent, or hostile father.) The boy needs to feel love from his father and needs to identify with him. It is through this male bonding that a child develops a sense of himself as an individual and as a male. If this relationship is not functional, the needs that would normally be met through it remain unmet.

This bonding may not occur if the father is physically or emotionally uninvolved in his child's life or the bond may be broken if he is punishing or authoritarian. Since this can be very painful, the child may not want to reestablish the connection. Even if the father tries to build a good relationship, the child may prevent it out of fear of further hurt. Dr. Elizabeth Moberly of Cambridge University refers to this as *defensive detachment*.[21] The child defends against further trauma by blocking himself from relating normally with his father, and in so doing, unknowingly insures that his needs for attachment will not be met. It becomes an approach-avoidance conflict. The drive for a renewed attachment shows his need for love from his father, but the defensive detachment prevents the attachment and so the needs continue unmet.

The child's interpretation of this relationship is critical. Even if the father is available and loves the child, if the child does not perceive that love or cannot connect with the father, there will be a deficit. There is a difference between *being* loved and *feeling* loved. The more sensitive the child and the more unable to relate to his father, the greater the chance of a relationship problem. To a child, the parent is his source of being, and if the attachment to the parent is disrupted, his very being feels endangered. The hurt child may become unwilling to trust and may learn to repress his need for attachment. He may then distance himself from his father and later carry it over to men in general by avoiding closeness with his male peers. Thus he becomes emotionally needful as a result of not having the supportive, affectionate relationships he requires to develop a good sense of identity. When these psychological needs remain unfulfilled, although the boy grows to be a man, he is still essentially a child trying to fill basic emotional needs. In many respects, he may still be a dependent child who needs to be loved by his father and not yet an adult with adult needs.

To learn more about the father-son relationship and defensive detachment, read Elizabeth Moberly's book *Homosexuality: A New Christian Ethic*

It should be emphasized that the deficit existed because the child could not connect with his father or didn't perceive that the relationship was what he desired. It doesn't necessarily mean that the father was detached or unloving—the father may have done everything in his power to develop a healthy, nurturing relationship.

Relationship with mother

The boy's relationship with his mother is also important. A mother can either reinforce and strengthen the boy's relationship with his father, or she can dominate and minimize the father's role. A strong relationship with the mother is not a problem unless it gets in the way of a strong relationship with the father. In the triangle of relationships between the boy, mother, and father the three sometimes become imbalanced. If the father-mother relationship is not healthy, the son misses out on learning what a husband-wife relationship should be. Further, the son may try to take care of the emotional needs of the mother and thus becomes a surrogate male companion to her. When this disordered mother-son relationship occurs, the boy does not develop a normal male image as a boy, nor are his emotional needs met as a son from his mother. Needless to say, he also does not get his emotional needs met from the father-son relationship. The boy becomes enmeshed with mom, in part to compensate for the fact that he does not have the emotional support from his father.[22]

Gender identity

As children develop, it is important to gain a healthy sense of who they are as a man or woman. In normal development, the concept of masculinity (what it means to be a man) is internalized before puberty by interaction with, and validation from, other boys and men. If a boy is confused about what it means to be a man or does not feel affirmed in his masculinity, he may internalize the concept of masculinity in unhealthy ways with frustrating results. When this happens, he typically will not realize that anything abnormal is happening. As he enters puberty and sexual feelings emerge, they may become confused with his masculine longings.

Having diminished feelings of masculinity does not mean he sees himself as feminine—that is the case for only a small percentage of men. There is a considerable difference between feeling inadequate as a male and feeling feminine. Many men who have homosexual feelings are masculine in appearance and action. They simply have not affirmed within themselves their validity as a man.

It is important to respect the divinely appointed roles that are uniquely male or female. But beyond that, there is great room to provide opportunities for children to develop talents in various directions unhindered by improper stereotypes.

Defensive detachment may also express itself in the development of gender identity. The effeminacy of some men with homosexual attractions and the quasi-masculinity of some women with homosexual attractions are examples of defensive detachments from the person's gender. They feel the need to identify with their own gender, but they reject it because they perceive it to be harsh or hurtful, and they prevent its normal development in a defensive way. In these cases, the development of their identity as male and female was likely stopped at an early stage of development.

Male emotional needs

A boy's need for the love and identification with other males is a normal, legitimate requirement every boy has. These needs are usually met by fathers or another significant male during early childhood and later reinforced by peers, teachers, and society as a whole. For many men with homo-sexual attractions, their perfectly natural needs for love, acceptance, and identification with other males were not fulfilled, and now because of their insecurities they do not venture out to legitimately fulfill them. They long for the companionship, love, and acceptance of their male peers, but when it is offered they resist because of fear of hurt or rejec-tion. They may then feel hurt that the opportunity for com-panionship and attention has passed them by. They may secretly fear they are not worthy of companionship or atten-tion and therefore stay where it is safe but lonely rather than venture out to interact with other men.

Many report that during childhood they felt different from their peers—loners who did not play the rough games that boys commonly play. Others had some friends, but wished for more and felt unable or unworthy of more substantial rela-tionships that were important to them. For these boys, their attraction to other males is rooted in the need to identify with and be accepted by other males and feel part of a group of buddies. At a time critical for making friends, their life may have been disrupted by a medical problem or a move to a new neighborhood, or overprotective parents may have interfered with peer relationships. Since they had limited contact with other boys, they did not identify with them in healthy ways, but anticipated rejection and expected they would not fit in. They desperately want acceptance and comfort from these ideal friends, but instead develop feelings of loneliness and longing.

Feeling alienated from the boys, they become attracted to them as an opposite. Watching from the sidelines, they admire the boys and wish they could be like them. Even as adults, they may be attracted to men who look or dress the way they wish they did. A man who is young and carefree may envy a professional who is responsible and mature. And the mature professional may wish he could be young and carefree.

This longing for a friend can be intense and can easily turn to adoration and idolization. As the boy enters puberty and sexual feelings emerge, this intense envy can turn to sexual lust, and if he is not able to fill his need for love and acceptance through brotherly relating, he may begin to seek it through sexual relating. The homosexual behavior may be an attempt to complete the person's masculine identity as he tries to possess valued masculine attributes through sexual intimacy with another male. It may be an effort to solve the mystery of masculinity that arises from the perception of being unlike other men. And it may also be a simple escape from his inadequacies and pain. In the heat of passion, one can momentarily believe any fantasy—that he is beautiful, masculine, loved, and accepted.

These underlying emotional needs are the same for all men, whether they have homosexual problems or not. The homosexual drive is actually a drive to fulfill the emotional need to relate to and be accepted by other men. "Love among those of the same sex is right and good," explain Drs. Thomas and Ann Pritt. "Only the sexualization of the attraction is inappropriate."[23] This attraction to other men is a reparative drive and is actually an attempt to resolve the problem, and not the problem itself. The core problem is not homo*sexual*, but homo*social*. It is a continual attempt to remedy earlier deficits and fulfill the social and emotional needs that still exist. The fulfillment of these unmet needs for love and identification can only be solved through nonsexual relationships with other men. The attractions will persist until he is able to develop a healthy identity and relate appropriately with other men in a nonsexual way.[24] Until these relationship needs are fulfilled, he is still essentially a child trying to fill basic emotional needs. He is still a boy who needs to identify with other boys.

Self-Worth

Low feelings of self-worth and inferiority are common breeding grounds for homosexual problems. Traumatic experiences in a child's life can lead to feelings of inferiority. Negative interactions with other boys can easily damage a vulnerable self-image and increase a boy's sense of being different from other children. This sense of feeling different is always a feeling of inferiority.

Many men who have homosexual attractions report feeling different and alone. Being different creates a mindset that has a tremendous impact on a person's development and on the way he understands the world. These feelings may separate him from his peers and he may feel that he lives his entire life from the outside looking in. Knowing that his attractions are not normal, he keeps them secret and this secret not only increases his sense of aloneness, but makes him feel he is of less value than other boys. Unfortunately, the feelings of isolation, inferiority, and fear of exposure are the very forces that keep the underlying issues from being re-solved. Other children may pick up on his sense of inade-quacy and attack it, causing him to withdraw further, defen-sively detach, and develop a fantasy life.

Even more dreaded than the attractions is the terrifying realization that the attractions are wrong—they are in conflict with his religious and moral beliefs. This creates a sense of shame, which is another proof to him that he is inferior in relation to other males. The feelings of being different, infe-rior, and guilty often lead to self-belittling and self-degrading thoughts. He may feel that he is inherently defective. The boy does not understand that his attractions are a result of a *deficit* and not a *defect*.

When young people reach puberty and find they don't have normal feelings toward the opposite sex, they are devastated. They try to live righteous lives and make the feelings go away, but the feelings don't go away. They grow up hating themselves and become convinced that others would also hate them if they were to find out these inner feelings. They begin to question the worth of living and thousands of young men commit suicide rather than be an awful, hated person who is attracted to his own sex.

Early Sexual Experiences

Children who have unresolved needs for affection or who experience social or emotional trauma can be particularly vulnerable to negative experiences. Early masturbation, exposure to pornography, or childhood sexual experimentation often introduce sexual thoughts before young men are able to understand them, and they can reinforce homosexual interests. Children who are victimized by sexual abuse or youth who have early sexual contacts can become confused and develop a gender misidentity and unusual sexual interests and values. Inappropriate sexual activity blurs the distinction between intimacy and sex.

Developmental conclusions

Many boys become aware of their same-sex attractions at an early age (sometimes before age five). The most important formative years for the development of sexual feelings and attitudes are during late infancy and before the onset of puberty, and not during puberty and adolescence. Dr. John Money explained, "The hormones of puberty activate what has already formed and is awaiting activation."[25] A child's development of heterosexual interests proceeds instinctively unless emotional maturity is obstructed by issues such as those just discussed. Dr. William Consiglio describes homosexuality as a *disorientation* from the mainstream of heterosexual development. "It is not something a person is born with; rather, it is sexual disorientation when the God-designed stream of heterosexuality is blocked. Homosexuality is not an alternative sexuality or sexual orientation, but an emotional disorientation caused by arrested or blocked emotional development in the stream of heterosexuality."[26] But the good news is that the condition is correctable. When these blockages are "successfully reduced, diminished, or removed, human sexuality can resume its natural heterosexual flow toward its proper, God-designed outlet; i.e., wholesome, mature, sexual, and emotional expression in marriage with a person of the opposite sex."[27]

The homosexual urge is not unrealistic or rebellious. It is not a fear of, or a flight from, heterosexuality. It is actually an unconscious attempt to fill normal emotional needs and when these needs begin to be filled, the person can begin again progressing toward full heterosexual maturation.[28]

Summary

Personality, genetics, and developmental experiences all have a place in influencing the development of homosexual attractions. Drs. Byne and Parsons at Columbia University believe it is important to "appreciate the complexities of sexual orientation and resist the urge to search for simplistic explanations, either psychosocial or biologic."[29] They emphasize that in addition to the influences of genetics or the environment, the individual plays an important role in determining his or her identity.

Dr. John Money stated, "Many wrongly assume that whatever is biological cannot be changed, and whatever mental can be. Both propositions are in error. Homosexuality is always biological and always mental, both together. It is mental because it exists in the mind. It is biological because the mind exists in the brain. The sexual brain through its extended nervous system communicates back and forth with the sex organs."[30]

Elder Dallin H. Oaks said that "some kinds of feelings seem to be inborn. Others are traceable to mortal experiences. Still other feelings seem to be acquired from a complex interaction of 'nature and nurture.' All of us have some feelings we did not choose, but the gospel of Jesus Christ teaches us that we still have the power to resist and reform our feelings (as needed) and to assure that they do not lead us to entertain inappropriate thoughts or to engage in sinful behavior."[31]

Can Homosexual Problems Be Resolved?

Many young men struggle to make sense of their homosexual attractions in light of the gospel. They have a testimony of the gospel, but they also know these feelings are very real and strong. They want to be righteous, but find that their attempts to live the gospel don't make the feelings go away. They are caught between the gospel which is right and the attractions toward men that are contrary to the gospel. Their response is to (1) try to suppress the feelings and live the gospel or (2) decide that the gospel does not fit in their life and pursue the attractions, thereby losing out on the blessings of the gospel. Suppressing the feelings does not make them go away. Suppression means a continual struggle where, at best, the person is celibate but miserable, and at worst, leads a double life by pretending to be a good member of the Church but secretly engaging in homosexual behavior. The only way to resolve the problem is to identify the needs that cause the attractions and fill them in legitimate ways.

This chapter addresses the reality of resolving homosexual problems. It gives a definition of what it means to resolve these problems, statistics on the numbers of people who have resolved them, and information about the time the process takes. Finally, it discusses the ultimate goal of doing all this work.

Is it possible to resolve these problems?

The world has defined concepts such as *homosexual* and *sexual orientation* and tells us that they are inborn and cannot be changed. Many people have bought into this theory and believe that a homosexual orientation is as genetic as race or left-handedness. They say that those who have changed are simply engrossed in a fantasy and that some day they will come back to reality and realize they are still homosexual.

Although these "pro-gay" arguments are complex and can appear logical, they have little credibility when viewed in the broader perspective of the eternal plan of salvation. To believe that God would give us problems that we could not overcome is to deny the power of the atonement and the omnipotence of God.

President Spencer W. Kimball taught, "After consideration of the evil aspects, the ugliness and prevalence of the evil of homosexuality, the glorious thing to remember is that it is curable and forgivable. The Lord has promised that all sins can be forgiven except certain ones enumerated, and this evil was not among those named. Thus it is forgivable if totally abandoned and if the repentance is sincere and absolute. Certainly it can be overcome, for there are numerous happy people who were once involved in its clutches and who have since completely transformed their lives."[32]

I personally attest that it is possible to diminish homosexual attractions, eliminate homosexual behavior, and lead a happy life in full alignment with the gospel. I know this because I have done it. I used to be conflicted by my feelings and tormented by my desires to act out. Now that I have resolved these issues, I feel peace and comfort as a whole person. And mine is not the only case. I personally know many other people and have read about hundreds more who have resolved significant problems and are now much happier and at greater peace with themselves and with God.

What does it mean to resolve these problems?

The process described in this booklet is *not* one of learning to suppress the feelings and control the behavior through willpower. The goal is to *resolve* the issues that created the homosexual attractions in the first place and that now continue to sustain them. A transition out of homosexuality might include the following:

♦ reducing or eliminating homosexual desires.
♦ eliminating homosexual behavior.
♦ developing a secure sense of self and male identity.

Desires

As men begin to resolve their homosexual issues, they note that their sexual attractions toward men significantly decrease. They may reach the point where they are no longer sexually attracted to men at all. Others may continue to be attracted to other men as strongly as before, but they can learn to cope with the attractions without being overwhelmed by them.

Many men still experience some attractions from time to time, but they are able to deal with them with a minimum of anxiety and they do not dominate their lives or behavior. Over time, the feelings diminish both in number and intensity until it becomes easy to dismiss these fleeting thoughts, much like they do any other unwanted thought that enters their minds. Most find that heterosexual feelings awaken or increase within them.

Behavior

With a greater understanding of their issues, men with homosexual struggles recognize that they can choose to avoid sexual activity with other men and most are able to control their actions. The comforting news is that as they resolve deeper issues, they find that their compulsions to act out diminish and in many cases disappear. As time passes, homosexual behavior becomes less and less appealing, and in some cases, even repulsive.

Those who have been heavily involved in sexual behavior for a number of years have a greater struggle overcoming

habits and sexual addictions. But if they are sincerely motivated and make a significant effort, they can overcome these
addictions.

Identity

Men are attracted to other men because of a distorted
view of themselves and others. If they have accepted a "gay"
identity, they can change that perception and accept themselves as sons of God with eternal potential. With increased
levels of self-acceptance, their feelings of self-worth and
masculinity will increase, they will begin to see their value in
relation to other men, and stop comparing themselves with
other men. As they become more pro-active rather than
reactive, they will be able to develop increasingly healthy
relationships with men and sexual attractions decrease.

How many people change?

Since homosexuality is the outward manifestation of
unresolved issues that are central to the individual's personality, deciding to work on these issues involves reevaluating his
core person and working to change it. This may be a long and
painful process, and not everyone who begins it sees it
through.

A person's success will vary because of several factors,
chief among which I believe is his level of commitment. There
is hope for those who are committed to the process and put
forth a significant effort. Although it was the hardest thing I
have ever done, it was worth the effort. I no longer struggle
with homosexuality. It no longer controls my life or domi-
nates my thoughts. For me to get to that point, it required the
following:

♦ personal study, prayer, pondering, and journaling over a
period of four years.

♦ building a closer relationship with my Heavenly Father

and Jesus Christ.

♦ reaching out and building important male relationships.

♦ individual therapy for five months.

♦ group therapy (two six-week groups).

♦ support group meetings for three and a half years.

Of those who make this kind of commitment, most are able to resolve their problems and make significant, long-lasting changes in their lives.

For more than seventeen years, Dr. William Consiglio has worked with men and women who seek freedom from homosexuality. He finds that 40% of his clients find personal resolution and enjoy a full heterosexual life, with many entering marriage and parenthood. Another 40% achieve a functional resolution in that they are able to control their homosexual thoughts, attractions, and behaviors, and thus maintain consistent celibacy. The remaining 20% drop out of the process and eventually return to active homosexuality.[34] He reports that even for those who do not make a complete heterosexual recovery there is great hope. They can "achieve a significant degree of emotional healing, growth in self-worth, and spiritual well being and are able to move on in life freed of the homosexual obsession and preoccupation. It allows them to form rewarding and fulfilling relationships and live more integrated and satisfying lives which are compatible with their spiritual values and convictions. And that's powerfully good news in itself."[35] Many other professionals report similar success rates.[36]

People typically keep homosexual issues to themselves and when they resolve their problems they move on quietly with their lives. Psychologist Gerard van den Aardweg said that cases of people who resolve their homosexual problems "are perhaps more numerous than we would presume, because many of them prefer to stay anonymous and not be public examples of 'the converted-and-cured-homosexual.'"[37]

How long does it take?

The length of the transition varies depending on the severity of the individual's problems, his level of motivation and commitment, and many other factors. Those who are able to define their problems and begin working on them early, before compulsive behaviors turn into addictions and before attitudes turn into identity, may be able to make the transition in a matter of months. Those who begin the process later in life after years of sexual habits and mental conditioning find it takes much work and substantially more time. Most men I have spoken with report it takes somewhere from three to ten years. However, don't set time frames and expect that changes will happen within a certain period of time. The problems didn't develop overnight and they likely won't be resolved in a short time.

The ultimate goal

The ultimate goal of this transition process is to achieve the following:

♦ a sense of belonging to the male gender.
♦ a comfortableness with heterosexual men.
♦ male relationships that are emotionally healthy.
♦ the ability to relate to women emotionally, spiritually, and physically.
♦ the ability to function effectively as a husband and father.
♦ the personal satisfaction of understanding, controlling, and feeling good about oneself.

How Can Homosexual Problems Be Resolved?

Choices

A man who has homosexual problems still has his agency and can make correct choices about his life. Although his freedom may be reduced because of susceptibilities or situations beyond his control, he must accept personal responsibility for his actions and the direction of his life. Satan would have him believe he is not responsible for his agency because he was "born this way" and has no control over his homosexual actions. Although he did not choose to have homosexual attractions, he *does* choose how to respond to them and his ability to resolve his homosexual problems will be determined by the control he decides to take over his life.

Accountability

He should identify those to whom he will be accountable:

♦ *To himself,* honestly admitting his problems and weaknesses.

♦ *To God* in daily prayer, confessing his weaknesses and asking for His strength to make it through the day.

♦ *To his bishop* or branch president for sins that should be confessed.

♦ *To his therapist* for how well he is following through on the things he needs to do.

♦ *To a confidant.* This may be someone who also has a personal struggle with homosexuality or simply a close friend.

Plan of action

With the counsel of his bishop and therapist, he should identify specific areas where work is needed to resolve problems. To repair and mature emotionally, he may need to come to grips with past emotional trauma, resolve current emotional conflicts, overcome emotional detachments and dependencies, learn to love appropriately, build healthy relationships, correct self-perceptions, or build feelings of masculinity and self-worth. To develop spiritually, he may need to learn to surrender to God, overcome envy and lust, give Christian service, or develop spiritual wholeness.

His efforts need to be kept in balance. If he spends too much time reading and studying about homosexual issues, he won't have time to build relationships. If he relies on support groups too much, he may not get individual therapy or focus on developing spiritually.

Multifaceted approach

A man can be more successful when he uses all the relationships and resources available, such as family, friends, counselors, Church leaders, faith, prayer, group and individual therapy, books, and support groups. He also needs to grow in other areas like coming to understand his true self, confirming his masculine identity, healing old wounds, forgiving, reconciling his relationship with his father or others, and learning to control his behavior. And most important, spirituality will need to play a major role. Commitment to and faith in Jesus Christ is the key to applying the healing power of the atonement in his life.

Personal study

One of the biggest challenges will be to overcome confusion by getting good, true information. Many men report this helps them make sense of their feelings and see things in a more enlightened perspective. A number of good books are listed at the end of this booklet.

Support groups

Most men find support groups to be very helpful. A support group should be a safe and confidential place where a man with homosexual problems can come to know he is not alone in his struggle. It is a place to find encouragement from other men who are working to resolve the same problems, and that will help reduce feelings of being alone, different, and isolated. He will discover that even when others know all about him, they still accept him. When feelings of rejection are gone, he finds he has the courage to relate to men in the group and eventually to men outside the group.

In addition to conventional support groups, experiential groups can be helpful. These groups provide a specific experience, such as sports programs that teach basic skills and provide opportunities to play the sport. Participants learn how to function on a team and have the chance to face and resolve old fears and feelings of rejection and feel accepted as a member of a team of men.

Support groups can also be helpful to wives, parents, siblings, and others who may need to work through their own issues.

Be careful to choose a support group that upholds the doctrines of the gospel, the scriptures, and the practices of the Church without reservation or exception. Steer clear of groups that seek to justify homosexual behavior or find exception with the doctrines or practices of the Church. Evergreen International is an umbrella organization that can give referrals to safe support groups and therapists. (Information on contacting Evergreen International is found at the end of this booklet.)

Therapy

Individual therapy is an essential part of the process for most men who resolve their homosexual problems. A trained therapist can help a man clarify his identity, make life choices consistent with his personal values, and guide him through the complex process of transitioning out of homosexuality. Group therapy can also be beneficial.

It is advisable that a man chooses a male therapist who can understand and support him in his personal values. An ideal counselor would be LDS or at least a man who upholds Christian values. Avoid "gay-affirmative" therapy, which encourages individuals to "come out of the closet" and accept homosexuality. This approach is not in harmony with gospel principles. Methods such as reparative, re-education, or reorientation therapies can help a man identify the source of his problems, develop a secure gender identity, and build healthy relationships with other men that diminish the sexual attractions he feels toward men.

Behavior

An important first step is to get homosexual behavior under control. A man who has been heavily involved in sexual activities may have a demanding struggle to overcome habits and sexual addictions. But if he is sincerely motivated and makes a significant effort, he can overcome them and control his behavior. The comforting news is that as he resolves deeper issues, the compulsions and desires to act out will diminish or disappear and the struggle to control his behavior will be less demanding. As time passes, homosexual behavior will become less and less appealing, and in some cases, even repulsive.

Self-Perception

A man's attractions are caused, in part, by his perception of the world and his instinctive efforts to become a part of something he knows he needs. Homosexuality is the story he tells himself to explain what he doesn't understand. If he has labeled himself a "homosexual," he has taken upon himself the extra baggage of society's definition of a homosexual. His task, then, is to discover what he doesn't understand and adjust his perceptions to match reality.

Self-image and self-worth

Homosexual problems have little to do with sexuality, but a lot to do with self-image (how a man thinks about himself) and self-worth (how he feels about himself). Many men who struggle with homosexual attractions have good self-images—they have good jobs and get along well in life. But they have low feelings of self-worth—their gut-level feelings tell them they are not worth much. A man may have to spend some time evaluating and correcting issues about his self-image.

Masculinity

A man who has homosexual problems may feel inadequate in his masculinity. Having diminished feelings of masculinity does not mean he sees himself as feminine or wishes he were a woman. There is a considerable difference between feeling inadequate as a man and feeling feminine. As a boy, he may not have fully internalized what it means to be a male or how to function as a male. He may not have had a nurturing relationship with his father or another significant male to feel fulfilled in his masculinity, and as a result may now need to do some work to make up for these deficits.

Emotions

Although a man may know he must overcome homosexual behavior and change his perception of himself, he needs to accept it emotionally and be willing to endure the pain that will inevitably come as his emotional child grows to an adult. He needs to learn to face his problems and deal with them directly. He must be emotionally open and honest with himself and with others. Only then can he work out past trauma, accept responsibility for his life today, and work to make a better future. Together with his therapist, he can determine what he needs to do to make up for missed emotional growth.

Relationships

Homosexual problems stem from relationship deficits and one of the keys to resolving the problems is to repair existing relationships and build healthy, emotionally-satisfying ones. Men who make the most progress in resolving their problems are those who build quality male relationships. If the man lacks confidence or experience, he may need to begin by building safe relationships with men in his support group, and when his confidence grows, move on to building deeper relationships with men at work and in his ward.

Spirituality

Many men who have homosexual problems are deeply spiritual men. Satan also recognizes this spiritual sensitivity and tries to use it against them. Tragically, their emotional needs are misdirected to homosexual feelings which may divert them from developing higher levels of spirituality. This is one of Satan's tools to rob the priesthood from the elect.

In his efforts to resolve his homosexual problems, it is important that a man recognizes the need to gain a greater understanding of basic gospel principles such as faith, the atonement, repentance, and forgiveness. Frank Worthen, a pioneer in Christian groups that minister to people with homosexual attractions, explained, "Our deliverance from homosexuality comes from a Person, rather than a method."[37] Personal growth and healing come as a man puts total faith in his Savior who has the power to change his life. There is no condition we could be born into that the Savior cannot repair. There is no condition that could obstruct our temporal and eternal happiness and potential that He cannot correct. And when a man has done all he can, the Savior will take it from there and do the rest.

───────────

This booklet is only a brief introduction to the subject of homosexuality. For further reading, see the books on the following pages. For personal help, see the listing of organizations on page 44.

Selected Readings

If you can't find these books at your local bookstore, you can order them conveniently and confidentially through the mail from Evergreen International or from Regeneration Books (see the Organizations section at the end of this booklet).

Resolving Homosexual Problems: A Guide for LDS Men, by Jason Park (Century Publishing, Salt Lake City, UT, 1997). This book explains same-sex attractions from a Latter-day Saint perspective and gives practical suggestions on how to resolve your homosexual problems. The companion book *Helping LDS Men Resolve their Homosexual Problems* is written to suggest to others how they may help the LDS man as he struggles with these issues.

Helping LDS Men Resolve their Homosexual Problems by Jason Park (Century Publishing, Salt Lake City, UT, 1997). This book explains same-sex attractions in a Latter-day Saint context and suggests how to help a man who is struggling to resolve his homosexual problems. It is written as a companion to *Resolving Homosexual Problems: A Guide for LDS Men*, which is written to the LDS man.

Understanding Male Homosexual Problems: An Introduction for Latter-day Saints by Jason Park (Century Publishing, Salt Lake City, UT, 1997). This short booklet gives a brief overview of the causes, challenges, and solutions to homosexual problems from a Latter-day Saint perspective.

A Place in the Kingdom: Spiritual Insights from Latter-day Saints about Same-Sex Attraction, edited by Garrick Hyde and Ginger Hyde (Century Publishing, Salt Lake City, UT, 1997). This book is a collection of life-story essays of men and women struggling with same-sex attraction, as well as spouses and parents. It provides both hope and perspective.

Born That Way? by Erin Eldridge (Deseret Book Company, Salt Lake City, UT, 1994). This LDS book describes a woman's personal struggle with same-sex feelings and how she overcame them through the power of Jesus Christ and by applying gospel principles.

Desires in Conflict: Answering the Struggle for Sexual Identity, by Joe Dallas (Harvest House Publishers, Eugene, OR, 1991). This Christian book provides practical, effective help for restoring sexual wholeness. It also provides information for family members and friends on how to give loving support and explains the rage felt by gay activists. The appendix gives answers to the pro-gay theology. Two chapters address lesbian concerns.

You Don't Have to be Gay, by J. A. Konrad (Pacific House Publishing, Newport Beach, CA, 1987). This easy-to-read book is written as a series of letters to a young man unfulfilled in his homosexuality. It teaches from a Christian perspective that people are not "born that way," that homosexuality is not a problem in relating to members of the opposite sex, and that homosexuality can be changed.

AMCAP Journal, vol. 19, no. 1–1993 (Association of Mormon Counselors and Psychotherapists, Salt Lake City, UT, 1993). This issue of the journal is devoted to the topic of homosexuality and contains articles, interviews and book reviews on homosexuality. It gives pertinent information about homosexuality from an LDS perspective.

Homosexuality: A New Christian Ethic, by Elizabeth R. Moberly (James Clarke & Co., Cambridge, England, 1983). A short, scholarly book on the root causes of homosexuality. Although hard for some to understand, this enlightening book states that the homosexual condition is an emotional and social problem, not just a sexual problem. It explains that the homosexual condition is a misguided attempt to fulfil normal developmental needs which for some reason were not fulfilled earlier. It distinguishes between the homosexual condition and its expression in homosexual activity.

Coming Out of Homosexuality: New Freedom for Men & Women, by Bob Davies and Lori Rentzel (Inter Varsity Press, Downers Grove, IL, 1993). This Christian book is written to people struggling with same-sex attractions. It provides straightforward ideas and helps.

Homosexual No More: Practical Strategies for Christians Overcoming Homosexuality, by Dr. William Consiglio (Victor Books, Wheaton, IL, 1991). Based on teachings developed for Christian ex-gay group meetings, this book identifies six stages of homosexual development and gives practical strategies for change, including principles of daily self-therapy.

Reparative Therapy of Male Homosexuality: A New Clinical Approach, by Joseph Nicolosi, Ph.D. (Jason Aronson, Inc., Northvale, NJ, 1991). Although written as a resource for therapists, this book can give insights and practical helps to those who struggle with homosexuality themselves. The book is helpful, readable, and consistent with general Christian teaching.

Understanding and Helping Those Who Have Homosexual Problems: Suggestions for Ecclesiastical Leaders (Church of Jesus Christ of Latter-day Saints, 1992, item number 32250). This booklet gives information to Church leaders on how to counsel and help.

Healing Homosexuality: Case Stories of Reparative Therapy, by Joseph Nicolosi, Ph.D. (Jason Aronson, Inc., Northvale, NJ, 1993). Personal testimonies from homosexual men who tried to accept a gay identity but were dissatisfied and then benefitted from psychotherapy to help free them from homosexuality. Offers insight to both therapists and patients who see homosexuality as a treatable condition. Discusses how group therapy heals and how reparative therapy works.

"Understanding Homosexuality and the Reality of Change" (Impact Resources, P.O. Box 1169, Murrieta CA 92564–1169, phone 800/333–6475). This sixty-minute video suitable for family viewing contains interviews with two men and two women on the roots of homosexual orientation and the change process, as well as interviews with therapists Joe Dallas and Joseph Nicolosi. This professional video is a valuable resource.

"Homosexuality: Hot Topics for Teens" (Media International, 313 E. Broadway, Suite 202, Glendale CA 91209, phone 800/477–7575). This is a fast-paced video is geared for teenagers. It is a shortened, sixteen-minute version of the video "Understanding Homosexuality and the Reality of Change." It includes a leader's study guide.

Homosexuality & Hope: A Psychologist Talks About Treatment and Change, by Gerard van den Aardweg (Servant Books, Ann Arbor, MI, 1985). This book states that homosexuality is a psychological problem that can be successfully treated. It discusses self-pity, inferiority complex, self-centeredness, and the value of humor. It states that homosexuality is not genetically based.

Organizations

Evergreen International, P.O. Box 3, Salt Lake City, UT 84110, phone 800/391–1000, Internet: http://www. evergreen-intl.org, e-mail: info@evergreen-intl.org. This nonprofit organization provides direction and support to Latter-day Saint men and women who want to diminish their same-sex attraction and free themselves from homosexual behavior. It is also a resource to family and friends, professional counselors, religious leaders, and all others who wish to help individuals who desire to change. The organization refers people to affiliated support groups and therapists, publishes manuals and newsletters, sells books by mail, and sponsors conferences. Call or write for a list of publications or information on a support group near you.

Regeneration Books, P. O. Box 9830, Baltimore, MD 21284–9830, 410/661–4337 or 410/661–0284. This mail-order organization sells many books written to a Christian audience. Call or write for a catalog.

Exodus International, P.O. Box 77652, Seattle, WA 98177–0652, phone 206/784–7799. This network of interdenominational Christian ministries offers support to men and women seeking to overcome homosexuality. Exodus maintains a referral list of ministries, churches, and individuals. It also publishes a newsletter and sponsors conferences. Call or write for an introductory packet of information.

Homosexuals Anonymous, P. O. Box 7881, Reading, PA 19603, phone 800/253–3000 or 610/376–1146. A nondenominational Christian organization that uses a modified twelve–step program modeled on that of Alcoholics Anonymous. The organization publishes a newsletter and other publications.

Sexaholics Anonymous, P. O. Box 111910, Nashville, TN 37222, phone 615/331–6230. A fellowship of men and women who want to stop their sexually self-destructive thinking and behavior. The philosophy and program is taken directly from the twelve steps and twelve traditions of Alcoholics Anonymous.

Family Research Council, 700 13th Street NW, Suite 500, Washington, DC 20005, phone 202/393–2100. The council is a research, resource, and educational organization that promotes the traditional family. It opposes gay marriage and adoption rights. It publishes numerous reports and newsletters from a conservative perspective on issues affecting the family.

Focus on the Family, 420 N. Cascade Avenue, Colorado Springs, CO 80903, phone 719/531–3400. A Christian organization that seeks to strengthen the traditional family. It has done research on homosexuality and school programs, civil rights laws, and other public policy questions. They publish numerous books and a monthly magazine.

National Association of Research and Therapy of Homosexuality (NARTH), 16542 Ventura Blvd., Suite 416, Encino, CA 91436, phone 818/789–4440. This nonprofit educational association is devoted to make effective psychological therapy available to all who seek to overcome homosexual problems. They conduct research and provide a referral service, lectures, and scholarly publications.

Notes

1   "Standards of Morality and Fidelity," letter from the First Presidency of the Church of Jesus Christ of Latter-day Saints, 14 Nov. 1991, numbering added.

2   "Standards of Morality and Fidelity," letter from the First Presidency of the Church of Jesus Christ of Latter-day Saints, 14 Nov. 1991.

3   "Same-Gender Attraction," Dallin H. Oaks, *Ensign*, Oct. 1995, p. 8.

4   "Reverence and Morality," Gordon B. Hinckley, *Ensign*, May 1987, p. 47.

5   "Standards of Morality and Fidelity," letter from the First Presidency of the Church of Jesus Christ of Latter-day Saints, 14 Nov. 1991.

6   "Standards of Morality and Fidelity," letter from the First Presidency of the Church of Jesus Christ of Latter-day Saints, 14 Nov. 1991.

7   "Stand Strong Against the Wiles of the World", Gordon B. Hinckley, *Ensign*, Nov. 1995, p. 99.

8   "Same-Gender Attraction," Dallin H. Oaks, *Ensign*, Oct. 1995, p. 13.

9   "Reverence and Morality," Gordon B. Hinckley, *Ensign*, May 1987, p. 47.

10 "Same-Gender Attraction," Dallin H. Oaks, *Ensign*, Oct. 1995, p. 13.

11 "Same-Gender Attraction," Dallin H. Oaks, *Ensign*, Oct. 1995, p. 13.

12 "Same-Gender Attraction," Dallin H. Oaks, *Ensign*, Oct. 1995, p. 14.

13 See *Resolving Homosexual Problems: A Guide for LDS Men*, Jason Park, Century Publishing, Salt Lake City, UT, 1997, pp. 11–13.

14 Figures used in this estimate: 5% of 10 million members of the Church equals 500,000 who have homosexual problems; 200,000 spouses (about 40% are or have been married according to NARTH survey results); 1,000,000 parents; 1,150,000 siblings (average 2.3 siblings per family in the Church according to a 1981 survey by the Church's Correlation Research Division); giving a total of 2.85 million. The figures for the United States would be 5% of 270 million equals 13.5 million; 5.4 million spouses; 27 million parents; 14.85 million siblings (average 1.1 per family according to "Family Life: Holding Together Better Than Most," *The Economist*, vol. 22, Feb. 1997, pp. 28–29.); giving a total of 60.75 million in the USA.

15 Cross-dressing is defined as wearing clothing or cosmetics usually deemed for the other gender, sometimes completely transforming themselves into the personae of the opposite gender. It goes beyond female impersonators ("drag queens") who dress up for money or attention. Cross-dressers get psychological relief or pleasure by playing the role of the opposite sex. It is estimated there are more than eight million cross-dressers in the United States—three to five percent of the general population.

16 *Homosexuality: A New Christian Ethic*, Elizabeth R. Moberly, James Clarke and Company, Cambridge, England, 1983, p. 3.

17 "Theories of Origins of Male Homosexuality: A Cross-Cultural Look," *Archives of General Psychiatry* 42, pp. 399–404.

18 "Same-Gender Attraction," Dallin H. Oaks, *Ensign*, Salt Lake City, Utah, Oct. 95, p. 9.

19 "Neurobiology and Sexual Orientation: Current Relationships," R. C. Friedman and J. Downey, *Journal of Neuropsychiatry* 5, 1993, p. 149.

20 For more information on these theories, see *Resolving Homosexual Problems: A Guide for LDS Men*, Jason Park, Century Publishing, Salt Lake City, UT, 1997, chapter two, or *Helping LDS Men Resolve their Homosexual Problems: A Guide for Family, Friends, and Church Leaders*, Jason Park, Century Publishing, Salt Lake City, UT, 1997, chapter two.

21 *Homosexual No More: Practical Strategies for Christians Overcoming Homosexuality*, Dr. William Consiglio, Victor Books, Wheaton, IL, 1991, p. 59.

22 *Homosexuality: A New Christian Ethic*, Elizabeth R. Moberly, James Clarke & Co., Cambridge, England, 1983, p. 6

23 For more information on these disordered relationships, you may refer to chapter four of *The Wonder of Boys* by Michael Gurian, audio book, Audio Partners Publishing Corp., Auburn, CA, 1996.

24 "Homosexuality: Getting Beyond the Therapeutic Impasse," Thomas E. Pritt, Ph.D. and Ann F. Pritt, M.S., *AMCAP Journal*, vol. 13, no. 1, 1987, p. 55.

25 See *Homosexuality: A New Christian Ethic*, Elizabeth R. Moberly, James Clarke & Co., Cambridge, England, 1983, p. 42.

26 *Gay, Straight, and In-Between*, John Money, Oxford University Press, New York, NY, 1988, p. 124.

27 *Homosexual No More: Practical Strategies for Christians Overcoming Homosexuality*, Dr. William Consiglio, Victor Books, Wheaton, IL, 1991, p. 22.

28 *Homosexual No More: Practical Strategies for Christians Overcoming Homosexuality*, Dr. William Consiglio, Victor Books, Wheaton, IL, 1991, p. 22.

29 See *Homosexuality: A New Christian Ethic*, Elizabeth R. Moberly, James Clarke & Co., Cambridge, England, 1983, chapter two.

30 "Human Sexual Orientation: The Biologic Theories Reappraised," William Byne and Bruce Parsons, *Archives of General Psychiatry* 50, Mar. 1993, pp. 236–37.

31 *Gay, Straight, and In-Between*, John Money, Oxford University Press, New York, NY, 1988, p. 123.

32 "Same-gender Attraction," Dallin H. Oaks, *Ensign*, Salt Lake City, Utah, Oct. 1995, p. 10.

33 *The Miracle of Forgiveness*, Spencer W. Kimball, Bookcraft, Salt Lake City, UT, 1969, p. 82.

34 "Counseling Overcomers: A Four-Focus Framework," an address by Dr. William Consiglio (18th Annual Exodus Conference). Also quoted by Bob Davies in "Mainstreamed Homosexuality," *Leadership*, Summer 1995, p. 82.

35 *Homosexual No More: Practical Strategies for Christians Overcoming Homosexuality*, Dr. William Consiglio, Victor Books, Wheaton, IL, 1991, p. 13.

36 See *Resolving Homosexual Problems: A Guide for LDS Men*, Jason Park, Century Publishing, Salt Lake City, UT, 1997, pp. 33–36.

37 *Homosexuality and Hope: A Psychologist Talks About Treatment and Change*, Gerard van den Aardweg, Servant Books, Ann Arbor, MI, 1985, p. 96.

38 *Coming Out of Homosexuality: New Freedom for Men & Women*, Bob Davies & Lori Rentzel, InterVarsity Press, Downers Grove, IL, 1993, p. 29.